the village where I was born, there was a old gardener who was wid
ow to be solitary and asocial. Each time I walked by the garden whe
old man worked each day, I would watch him surreptitiously. You m
ow what I mean: I would glance sideways, like someone trying to see
swers on someone else's copybook. My eyes would hurt with the stra
so wanted to get a close look at him. But despite my curiosity, I wo
ways walk by as quickly as I could. The children in the village all h
es to tell on his account, so-called stories verified by an uncle,
andfather or an elderly aunt. Some said the old man was really an og

ers ight
s a e a
at was
uste I h
ver day
cide ; pl
se oint
dde lowe
ses, nee
ate ; c
s o ts
em rac
ces cho
rd: g

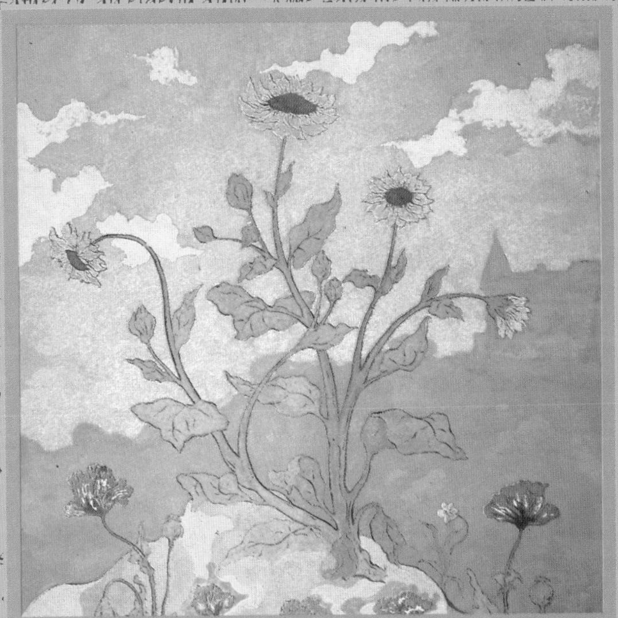

er was working, cutting here, raking there. I could see his face and
ckled and wrinkled skin, much like an overdone pancake left to cool
itchen counter. His lips moved constantly, as if he were conversing c
ntly with himself. The more I looked at him, the less threatening
med. How could a man who surrounded himself with so many flowers
ly dangerous? His garden was not very big; soon, he drew close to
mpletely unaware of my presence. Distinctly, I heard him speak.
s speaking to his flowers! I turned away, eager to stifle my bubb

n the village where I was born, there was a old gardener who was wid
ow to be solitary and asocial. Each time I walked by the garden wh
old man worked each day, I would watch him surreptitiously. You m
ow what I mean: I would glance sideways, like someone trying to see
swers on someone else's copybook. My eyes would hurt with the stra
so wanted to get a close look at him. But despite my curiosity, I wo

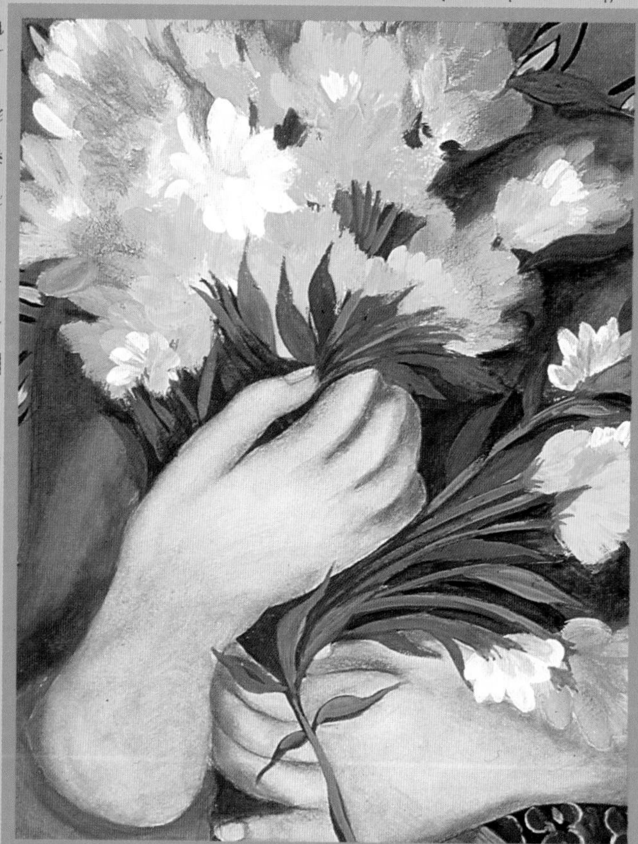

ntly with himself. The more I looked at him, the less threatening
med. How could a man who surrounded himself with so many flowers
y dangerous? His garden was not very big; soon, he drew close to
npletely unaware of my presence. Distinctly, I heard him speak. He
aking to his flowers! I turned away, eager to stifle my bubbling lau

Dreams of
Flower Gardens

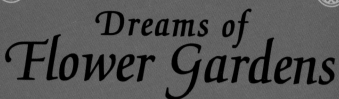

This book belongs to

_____

© 2000 Modus Vivendi Publishing Inc.
All rights reserved.

Published by:
Modus Vivendi Publishing Inc.
3859, Laurentian Autoroute
Laval, Quebec
Canada H7L 3H7
or
2565 Broadway, Suite 161
New York, New York 10025

Graphic Design: Marc Alain
Translation: Brenda O'Brien
Photo Credits:
Cover 1: ©Bibliothèque Forney/SuperStock; Cover 4: ©SuperStock
Page 1: ©Christie's Images/SuperStock; Page 2: ©Kactus Foto,
Santiago, Chile/SuperStock; Pages 3 and 5: ©Josephine
Trotter/SuperStock; Page 48: ©Christie's Images/SuperStock

Legal Deposit: 2nd Quarter, 2000
National Library of Canada
Cataloguing in Publication Data
Desbois, Hervé
 Dreams of flower gardens
 (Heartfelt Series)
 Translation of: Rêves de fleurs et jardins.
 ISBN 2-89523-022-6
 1. Gardens. 2. Flowers. 3. Gardens – Pictorial works.
 4. Flowers – Pictorial works. I. Title. II. Series.
SB450.98.D4713 2000   635.9'022'2   C00-940562-3

Canada We acknowledge the support of the Government of Canada through the
Book Publishing Industry Development Program for our publishing activities.

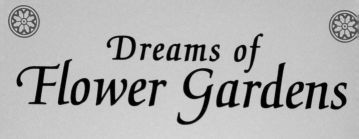

Dreams of Flower Gardens

Hervé Desbois

MV Publishing

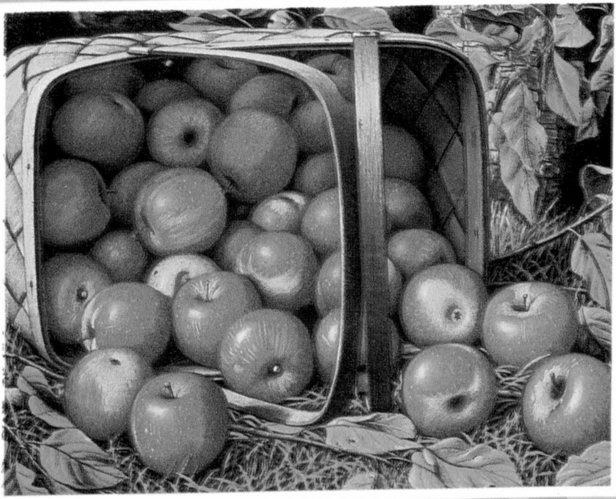
© Christie's Images/SuperStock

"Too many flowers blossom without ever being seen."
Anonymous

This little book is about the beauty and wonder of flowers and flower gardens. It contains no technical jargon, no fancy advice from horticultural experts. Instead, it is meant to warm the heart and rekindle the soul like the scent of flowers on a warm summer breeze.

Close your eyes and think of flowers in full bloom. Imagine your own beautiful flower garden. Can you see things with the eyes of a poet, of a lover of Nature? After all, the life of a flower begins with love. The seed sown in the soil bears this love and swells with desire. It desires to be seen and nurtured. It wishes to spread its beauty to the eyes of the beholder. Perhaps this is the secret of the beauty of flowers.

As we strive to cope with fast-paced modern life and the minor tribulations of the day-to-day, we need not forget the beauty and wonder that surrounds us. Just beyond our immediate vision is a whole world waiting to welcome us, open-armed. This is the gift of Mother Nature. The gift of life. The gift of rest. The gift of peace and contemplation. Look out beyond the chatter and noise of modern life and see that there is a whole world of wonder there waiting to welcome and console you.

"The Earth's poetry never ceases."
John Keats

This Spring, my grade school class was involved in a gardening project. Each child wrote a poem describing his or her experience. The result was very refreshing!

F is for flowers.

L is for little.

O is for outstanding.

W is for wonderful.

E is for everlasting.

R is for roses.

S is for sweet.

by Sam and Kailea

D is for dandy.

A is for a pretty flower.

I is for I planted a flower.

S is for sunny day.

Y is you've got to plant a flower!

by Taylor and Sammi

R is for reach for them but watch out for thorns

O is for open eyes that see the beauty

S is for a gift for someone special like Mom

E is for elegant and everlasting

S is sending flowers with a note to someone you love.

by Ben and Jack

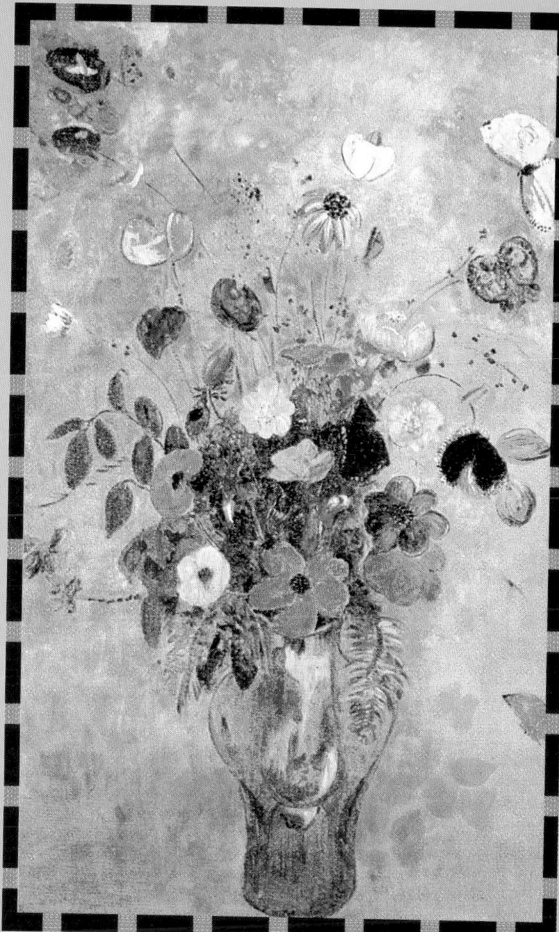

"Each of us must cultivate a secret garden."

Voltaire

In the village where I was born, there was a old gardener who was widely known as a hermit. I used to walk by the garden where the old man worked each day and watch him inconspicusously. You must know what I mean: I would glance sideways, like someone trying to see the answers on someone else's copybook. My eyes would hurt with the strain. I so wanted to get a close look at him. But despite my curiosity, I would always walk by as quickly as I could.

The children in the village all had tales to tell on his account. Some said the old man was really an ogre, others claimed he was the reincarnation of Bluebeard, others thought he was a bloodthirsty bandit and thief.

None of us knew what was true, but we all agreed on one thing: the old gardener was a monster, a cannibal, someone to keep away from at all costs!

Still, I had never seen the old man being mean to any one of us. And one day, I decided to take a closer look at him. This time, I found a hiding place close to his tool shed, at the back of his garden.

From my vantage point, I suddenly discovered a splendid garden filled with vegetables and flowers. Roses, tomatoes, marigolds, lettuce, pansies and cucumbers combined to create a symphony of dazzling colour. There were flowers everywhere; carpets of white, pink or purple along each row, tight-woven bouquets that seemed to explode into multicoloured bunches, climbing plants embracing fences, heavy with white and violet flowers. It reminded me of my schoolyard: quiet, yet likely to erupt at any minute. Meanwhile, the elderly gardener was working, cutting here, raking there. I could see his face and his speckled and wrinkled skin, much like an overdone pancake left to cool on a kitchen counter. His lips moved

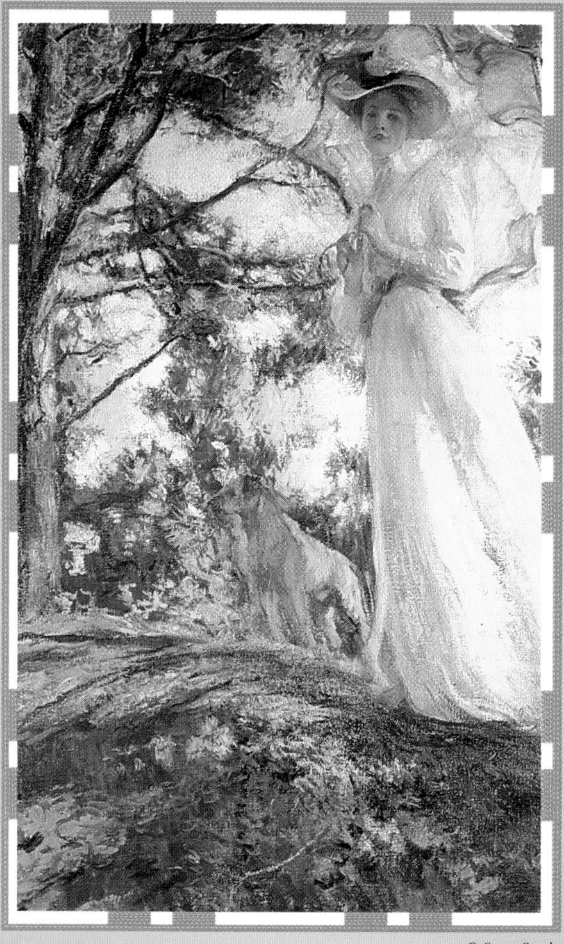

constantly, as if he were conversing with himself. The more I looked at him, the less threatening he seemed. How could a man who surrounded himself with so many flowers be truly dangerous?

His garden was not very big; soon, he drew close to me, completely unaware of my presence. Distinctly, I heard him speak. He was speaking to his flowers! I turned away, eager to stifle my bubbling laughter. But the old gardener spotted me and quickly began rushing toward me. I stood stock-still; my mind was filled with horror stories, I expected the very worst. But the old man spoke to me softly:

"Well! It isn't every day that someone comes to visit. Come in, come in. You seem to like my garden. Don't be afraid. I'll give you a guided tour."

He took me the hand and I followed him willingly.

"You see those miniature suns, near the green beans, that's camomile. This here is millefeuille, very good for soothing scratches and cuts. The flowers you see over there are foxglove, majestic but sharp and ready to bite. Touch them with your eyes only, they can be poisonous!"

With all the innocence of childhood, I asked him the question I so longed to have answered:

"So, after all, you aren't an ogre — am I right?"

The old gardener simply smiled.

"Do you know why I love flowers so much? Because they are uncomplicated. You see, even if they could speak, they would not judge me. And if they had eyes, they would see only an old gardener who loves them. A great many people should use them as a role model, don't you think? A great many people say stupid and thoughtless things. A great many people should learn to keep quiet."

Then he looked into my eyes, smiling, and winked.

"But you, you aren't one of those people, I can see that in your eyes. You're like me, you love flowers too."

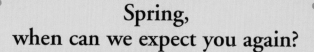

Spring,
when can we expect you again?

After months of blustery winter, now comes the season of rebirth. The earth shakes off its months of quiet hibernation and little by little, life finds renewed strength. The grey snow is giving way to timid colours, the glacial winds grow soft and fragrant. Nature once again prepares to display all its riches, slowly and steadily. To begin, a few snowdrops and multicoloured crocuses are stretching their tiny blooms toward the rays of April's timid sun. Then jonquils bloom like so many suns and narcissuses shine with white and gold. Here comes the hyacinths, the tulips and a myriad of other flowers eager to join in the dance.

Given such an exuberance of colours and fragrances, why not pick a bouquet to brighten our homes. The following are a few tips to help you make your blooms last as long as they possibly can:

♣ Before putting your flowers in a vase, cut their stalks diagonally, holding them under water; let tips soak for a few minutes to prevent air bubbles from entering the stalks.

♣ Remove any leaves below the water line.

♣ A few drops of leaves prevents the vase water from deteriorating; add food designed for cut flowers. Add a cup of any transparent soft drink to keep your flowers perky!

♣ Change the vase water two to three times a week. Do not wait until the water becomes murky or smelly. When you change the water, clip the stalks again, diagonally.

♣ To prevent the growth of bacteria, it is very important to clean the vase thoroughly each time you

change the water. Remember to wash the vase in hot water and do not use soap.

♣ When the weather is very hot, add a few ice cubes to the vase water.

♣ As flowers begin to wilt, remove them from the bouquet.

♣ To keep your lilac bouquet beautiful for as long as possible, cut the stalks in two, lengthwise, and flatten them. The process helps lilacs absorb a maximum quantity of water.

The Language of Flowers

Not all of us understand the language of flowers in exactly the same way. When you send flowers to someone, avoid confusion by accompanying your bouquet with a written note! After all, the best way to understand one another is to talk (or to listen)! Although subject to debate, the following are a few interpretations regarding the language of flowers.

Aster: confident love.

Anemone: expectation, perseverance.

Gladioli: a rendezvous.

Hyacinth: heartfelt joy, loyalty.

Iris: good news, beauty, a tender heart.

Jasmine: voluptuous love, kindness.

Lavender: tenderness.

Lilac: friendship, first love.

Lily: fragility, royalty, purity.

Lily of the valley: good luck, discreet coquetry.

Pansy: affection.

Peony: sincerity.

Pink rose: friendship, sympathy, sensual delight.

Red rose: love, hope, encounters, passion.

Tulip: timidity, unconditional love.

Violet: modesty, propriety, secret love.

"Give me a land of boughs in leaf,
A land of trees that stand;
Where trees are fallen there is grief;
I love no leafless land."

A.E. Houseman

"The day I see a leaf is a marvel of a day."

Kenneth Patton

"Come sit on my porch and sip some tea, while we talk about friends and hollyhocks and laugh till dark as we watch the world go by."

Lyndsey Jones

"I know a little garden close,
Set thickly with lily and red roses.
Where I would wonder if I might,
From dewy morn to dewy night."

William Morris

"And when thou art weary,
I'll find thee a bed
of mosses and flowers
to pillow thy head."

John Keats

"Kiss of the sun for pardon.
Song of the birds for mirth.
You are closer to God's heart in a garden
than any place on earth."

Dorothy Frances Gurney

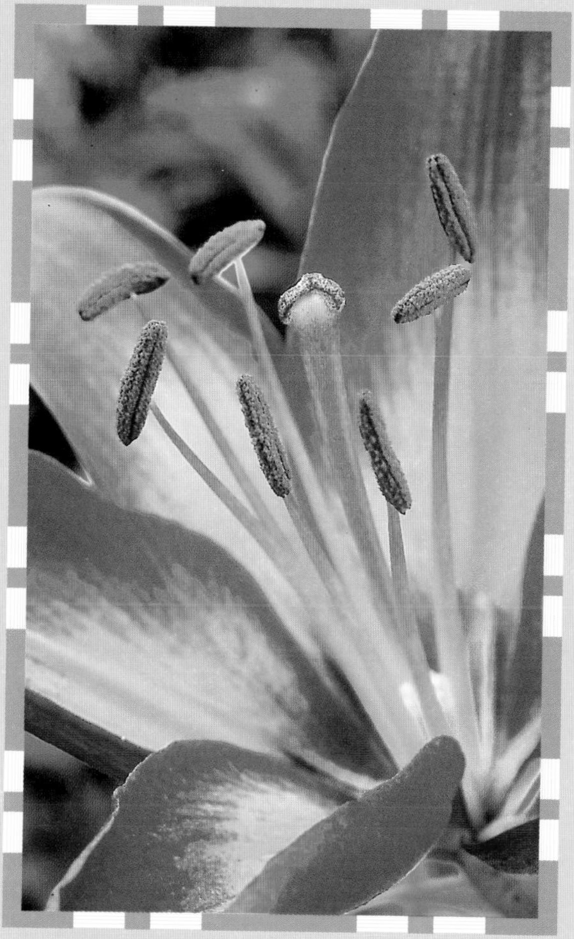

The Easter Flower

Far from this foreign Easter damp and chilly
My soul steals to a pear-shaped plot of ground
Where gleamed the lilac-tinted Easter Lily
Soft-scented in the air for yards around;

Alone, without a hint of guardian leaf!
Just like a fragile bell of silver rime,
It burst the tomb for freedom sweet and brief
In the young pregnant year at Eastertime;

And many thought it was a sacred sign,
And some called it the resurrection flower;
And I, in wonder, worshipped at its shrine,
Yielding my heart unto its perfumed power.

by Claude McKay

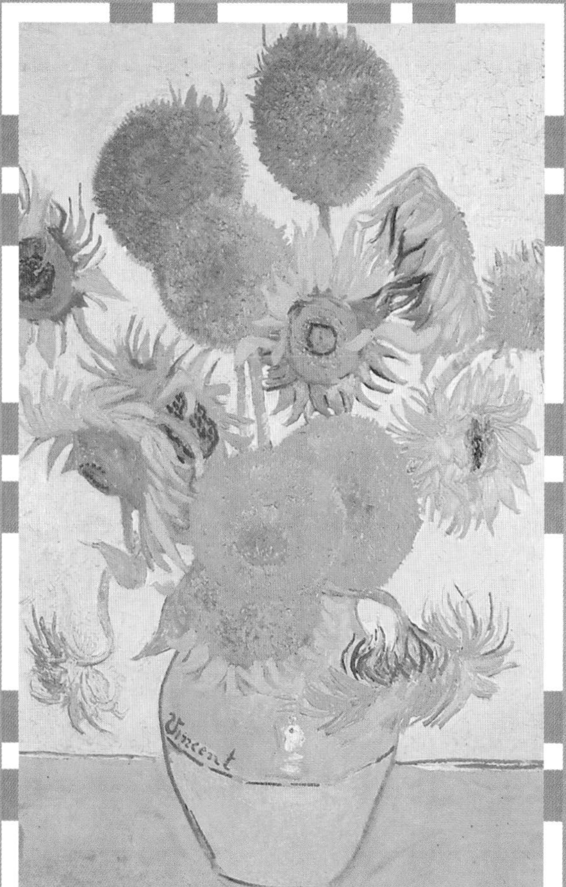
Vincent

"All of the flowers of the future are held in the seeds of today."

Chinese proverb

In the beginning, all was darkness. Still, I was well, I felt confident. I was neither cold nor hot, and I felt self-reliant. I am tempted to say that nothing was happening — but if I did so I would be lying. In truth, many things were happening, especially within my inner self. Dreams, dreams and dreams again. Some claim that dreams sow the seeds of life. I believe they are right. And those who believe they are wrong, or those who have simply ceased to believe, may be already dead in some sense.

And so these dreams swept through my existence and occupied a great deal of my time. Or should I say that I encouraged them and did nothing to eliminate them from my life. On the contrary! They would arrive without warning: a lightning flash, a sudden idea, a small seed begging for nourishment. And I? I nourished them with all of my illusions, deeply, freely, eagerly.

Though my dreams took on different forms, they remained the same. A cloud carried by the winds remains a cloud as long as it travels through the sky. Of course, I saw myself as beautiful and loved. Admired, but never to excess, respected for my true self, loved for what I truly was. I saw myself as admirably adorned, dressed in the most beautiful of clothing, bathed in the sweetest of perfumes. Alas, I am vain. I also saw myself dancing on summer nights, swaying in soft and refreshing breezes, bowing gracefully to my partners. Now had come my turn to be loved, with a tender and passionate heart. Now had come the time for me to embrace life!

How very simple it all seemed! I was convinced I could live on love alone, as they say! The sun was my friend, the wind, my confidant, my poet, and the water I drank was for me a source of calm and well-being. Yet, deep inside, I sensed that life brings to each of us stormy and empty passages. Still, I was certain that in difficulty I could also find growth — as long as I refused to dwell on my misfortune. I resolved to find strength in my moments of anger, discouragement, doubt and conflict. I pledged not to let negative circumstances control my life.

Then, one day, the ultimate event occurred in my life. Although my dreams played a major role in my life until the very end, nevertheless I felt that major changes had taken place within me; I am referring mainly to changes that were physical, increasingly significant and increasingly rapid. Such is life. Nothing is immutable; everything changes, everything evolves. The fledgling grows and leaves the nest, the green leaf emerges from its bud, and the butterfly eagerly escapes from its cocoon and flies happily away. And so, in my turn, I entered into the eternal dance of life. And believe it or not, I became my own dreams. I found a new existence, I found fulfilment, yet I sensed no need to hurry. I reached higher limits in grace and beauty, proudly but with no vanity, strongly but with no violence, intent on serving as a model but in no way desirous of creating envy in others.

I became royal, I became a flower, I became a rose.

"In everything governed by Nature, never is there an element of hurriedness."

Lamarck

There are an infinite number of publications which provide a practical approach to gardening and flowers. However, why not take a look at a few ideas, random musings and judicious advice gleaned from several sources? What better way to combine pleasure and practicality!

Nature is patient...
Although most of us are all too eager to plant seeds and flowers at the earliest sign of Spring, it is very important to remember to clean flower boxes thoroughly before using them again. Wash them with soapy water and ideally, disinfect them using a mixture of bleach and water. Rinse them well before filling them with soil.

To avoid drowning your plants with excess water, make sure your flower boxes drain efficiently. Line bottoms with fine gravel or clay and cover with any type of discarded fabric. The combination will facilitate water drainage.

Success is a day-to-day effort...
Regularly removing wilted flowers is a key element in gardening. While keeping your garden pretty, it is also an excellent way to encourage second or even third blooms.

The more your plants need water, the more they need fertilizer as well: in very warm weather, add a liquid fertilizer, once a week, to the water you sprinkle on them.

Plants can also suffer from too much watering. Before you water them, check to see if they really need it. Always try to water your garden and plants in the evening. If you can't, water in the very early morning.

Colours and tastes...
Annuals can add a great deal of colour to your garden. To avoid mixes that could be disappointing, choose two to three colours likely to create both harmony and contrast. Limit the number of colours and focus on different shapes and heights.

While you may not be an expert in colour coordination, you can use a few easy-to-follow rules. As interior decorators do, concentrate on the three primary colours: red, yellow and blue, and blend them to create secondary colours: red + yellow: orange; yellow + blue: green, blue + red: purple.

Colours not used to create secondary colours are complementary and will create a contrasting effect; for example, red and green. For a softer effect, combine colours that are similar in hue, such as red, orange and yellow. Of course, remember that the intensity of each colour is an important consideration. Trust your judgement and your taste!

"Had God not created woman, He would not have created the flower."

Victor Hugo

"I perhaps owe having become a painter to flowers."
Claude Monet

"I'd rather have roses on my table than diamonds on my neck."

Emma Goldman

"Where flowers bloom so does hope."
Lady Bird Johnson

"Each flower is a soul opening out to nature."
Gérard De Nerval

"They are not long, the days of wine and roses:
Out of a misty dream
Our path emerges for a while, then closes
Within a dream."

Ernest Dowson, 1867-1900

"Different flowers look good to different people.
Pick the flower when it is ready to be picked.
The flower that you spent time to care for does not grow,
While the willow that you accidentally planted
Flourishes and gives shade."

Chinese proverb

The Rose of Life

A certain man planted a rose and watered it faithfully, and before it blossomed, he examined it.

He saw the bud that would soon blossom and also the thorns. And he thought, "How can any beautiful flower come from a plant burdened with so many sharp thorns?"

Saddened by this thought, he neglected to water the rose, and before it was ready to bloom, it died.

So it is with many people. Within every soul there is a rose. The God-like qualities planted in us at birth grow amid the thorns of our faults.

Many of us look at ourselves and see only the thorns, the defects. We despair, thinking that nothing good can possibly come from us.

We neglect to water the good within us, and eventually it dies. We never realize our potential.

Some people do not see the rose within themselves; someone else must show it to them.

[...] Our duty in this world is to help others by showing them their roses and not their thorns.

Only then can we achieve the love we should feel for each other; only then can we bloom in our own garden.

Author Unknown

Was there ever an ear as attentive as to hear a rose as it wilts?

There she stood, as pale as the dawn. Her huge, little girl's eyes betrayed all of her sadness.

"What is wrong?" I asked her.

Instead of answering, she ran her fingers through my hair. Unthinking, with no sign of the slightest shyness.

"Why are you sad?"

She still refused to answer, but in her eyes, I could read her story. We had come to know one another in the very early summer, well before the sun's rays were at their strongest. I forget which of us was first aware of the other's existence. All it takes is one look, a shadow of a smile, to create the first path that unites two souls. As I recall, this is precisely what happened on a morning in the month of June.

I was new in the neighborhood and I encountered many children, especially in the morning and the late afternoon. I would stand in front of my home, on a tiny piece of grass overlooking the sidewalk. On this particular morning, she walked by, humming quietly. Suddenly, she stopped. She looked up at me and gleefully cried: "This is the last day of school!" Then she went on her merry way. Towards the end of the same day, she passed by me once again, grinning from ear to ear. As I strolled by, she waved.

Then came the real summer season. Of course, school always ends as summer begins. Cynthia — that was her name — often dropped by to see me, even though she no longer had to walk to school. She was seven years old and she would willingly spend a long time telling me this and that. At her age, imagination is limitless, clear, and so refreshing, the very source of Life itself. I grew accustomed to Cynthia and Cynthia grew accustomed to me.

We began to get used to seeing one another, we failed

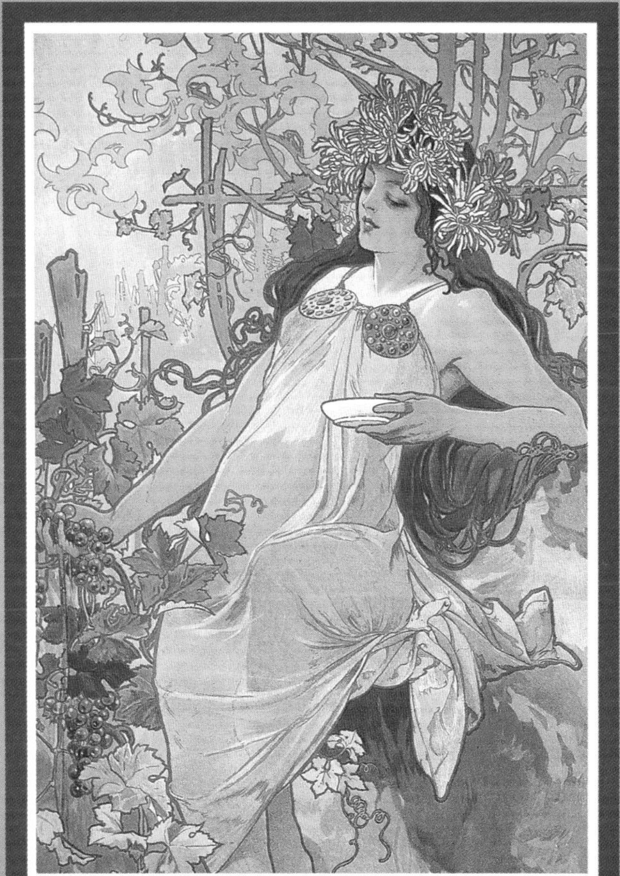

to see the days go by. But time takes with it child-hood and beauty, and all that we neglect to protect.

"I don't want you to die," she eventually said.

"Death is part of life," I replied.

Instinctively, I knew that I had given her the wrong answer.

"When I die, I will start a voyage that will bring me back to you."

"Will you come back next year?"

"Of course! I may not be the person you know now, but I will be more beautiful and stronger too. You know, we have to learn to die if we want to be reborn."

"Like a caterpillar that becomes a butterfly?"

"Exactly! You see, those who are too attached to what they already are can't see what they could become. And they die anyway!"

"But I'm not a butterfly; I'm not a flower."

"What you say is true. But each living being, in its own special way, follows the same path. You, for example, are neither your father nor your mother. Yet you are a bit of both, even though you are yourself. And the same pattern will continue if ever you become a mother yourself."

Cynthia took my head in her tiny hands. My petals, already battered by heavy rain and the hot sun, were still as soft as velvet on her cheeks. Cynthia began to hum softly. Her sadness had disappeared, even though I sensed the melancholy of two friends about to leave one another.

"Sleep, small flower, and dream of vivid colours to wipe away the too-white winter."

Cynthia caressed my tired head once again. She moved away from me, gazing lovingly at me one last time. The last image I had was Cynthia returning on her way to school, in the wonderful white world of the winter's first snow.

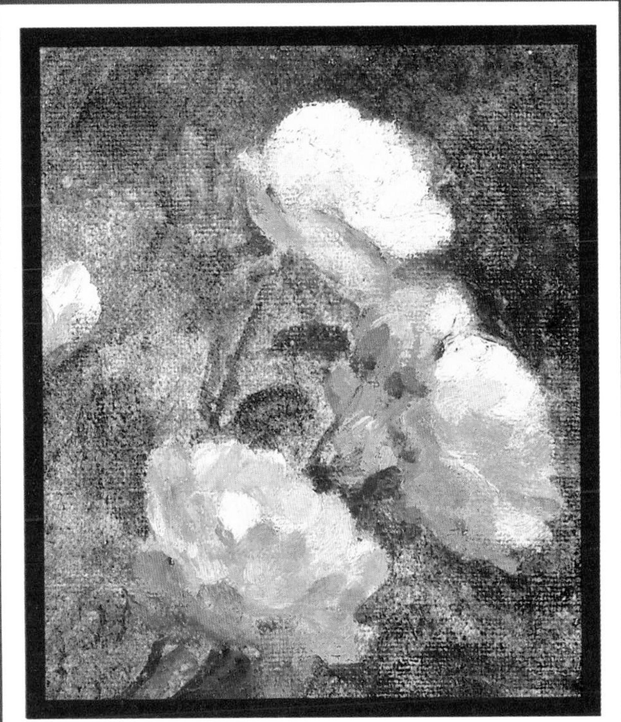

© Kactus Foto, Santiago, Chile/SuperStock

Nature and the Dinner Table

Edible flowers are flowers that you can enjoy in several ways. They can be served in salads and desserts, used to flavour vinegars, or added to syrups or jellies. They can also be used to decorate your culinary masterpieces.

Before eating them, make sure that flowers are edible and that they entail no risk whatsoever to your health. Some varieties belonging to the same species can be toxic, though others are not. Ask for details when you buy plants and seeds. And avoid chemicals!

Pick flowers that have bloomed recently, preferably early in the morning, when the weather is dry and once the morning dew has evaporated. Rinse them gently under cool water and look for any insects. Before eating them, remove any pistils and stamens and any white portions found at the base of petals.

If you do not intend to eat them immediately, edible flowers can be stored in the refrigerator for 24 hours, in a glass or plastic receptacle or in water. However, certain preparations require immediate use: oils and vinegars, for example.

Rose Petal Jelly

Rose petals, water and sugar in equal parts, pectin. Verify the quantity of water required by the pectin sachets (or for the pectin leaves). For example, one 7-gram package of pectin requires 500 ml of water, or two cups. In this instance, you will need 2 cups of rose petals, 2 cups of water and 2 cups of sugar.

- Bring the water to a boil, add the sugar, stir; add the rose petals.
- Let boil for 15 minutes.
- Let cool. Remove petals.
- Add pectin (follow package instructions).

For decorative purposes, add two or three petals to each jar of jelly.

Candied Violets

Remove the green portion at the base of each petal. Beat one egg white and dip each violet in the mixture (use eyebrow tweezers); dip each petal in icing sugar. Let dry and store away from light, in glass containers. These wonderful items are ideal for decorating cakes and are delicious when eaten as candies!

"And it is my faith, that every flower
Enjoys the air it breathes."

William Wordsworth

"Flowers leave some of their fragrance in the hand
that bestows them."

Chinese proverb

"I have a garden of my own,
But so with roses overgrown,
And lilies, that you would it guess
To be a little wilderness."

Andrew Marvell

"Footfalls echo in the memory
Down the passage which we did not take
Towards the door we never opened
Into the rose garden."

T.S. Eliot, Four Quartets

"All the flowers of all the tomorrows are in the seeds
of today."

Indian Proverb

"I frequently tramped eight or ten miles through the deepest snow to keep an appointment with a beech-tree, or a yellow birch, or an old acquaintance among the pines."

Henry David Thoreau, 1817-1862

"Keep a green tree in your heart and perhaps a singing bird will come."

Chinese proverb

"O chestnut tree, great rooted blossomer,
Are you the leaf, the blossom or the bole?
O body swayed to music, O brightening glance,
How can we know the dancer from the dance."

William Butler Yeats

"A man is a bundle of relations, a knot of roots,
Whose flower and fruitage is the world."

Ralph Waldo Emerson

"He that planteth a tree is a servant of God, he provideth a kindness for many generations, and faces that he hath not seen shall bless him."

Henry Van Dyke

"Find the seed at the bottom of your heart and bring forth a flower."

Shigenori Kameoka

"Happiness held is the seed; Happiness shared is the flower."

Anonymous

Oh, my love is like a red, red rose
That's newly sprung in June
Oh, my love is like a melody
That's sweetly played in tune
As fair art thou, my bonnie lass,
So deep in love am I
And I will love thee still, my dear,
Till all the seas gang dry.
Till all the seas gang dry, my dear,
Till all the seas gang dry
And I will love thee still, my dear,
Till all the seas gang dry.

'Til all the seas gang dry, my dear
And the rocks melt with the sun
And I will love thee still, my dear
While the sands of life shall run
But fare thee well, my only love
Oh, fare thee well a while
And I will come again, my love
Though t'were ten thousand mile
Though t'were ten thousand mile, my love
Though t'were ten thousand mile
And I will come again, my love
Though t'were ten thousand mile.

Robert Burns

he village where I was born, there was a old gardener who was wie
w to be solitary and asocial. Each time I walked by the garden where
man worked each day, I would watch him surreptitiously. You m
w what I mean: I would glance sideways, like someone trying to see
wers on someone else's copybook. My eyes would hurt with the strain
wanted to get a close look at him. But despite my curiosity, I wo
ays walk by as quickly as I could. The children in the village all h
s to tell on his account, so-called stories verified by an uncle, a gran

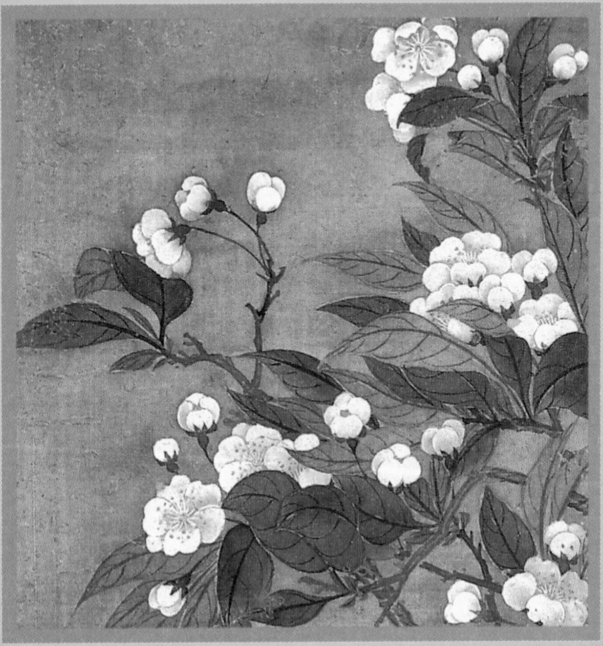

ner ... re, c
clai ... he w
ood ... ld w
fa ... rous
ann ... l ne
n th ... idea
e a ... his
d, o ... ly e
eree ... , tow
, m ... a sy
ny ... f wh
or ... exple
mul ... ith w
l vie ... ikely
pt a ... cut

, raking there. I could see his face and his speckled and wrinkled sk
h like an overdone pancake left to cool on a kitchen counter. His
ed constantly, as if he were conversing constantly with himself.
e I looked at him, the less threatening he seemed. How could a man w
rounded himself with so many flowers be truly dangerous? His gare
not very big; soon, he drew close to me, completely unaware of
sence. Distinctly, I heard him speak. He was speaking to his flowers
ned away, eager to stifle my bubbling laughter. But the old garde